# THE BEST EVER
# DEMOTI
## FOR HUMAN RESOURCE MANAG

*How To Dismay, Dishearten and Disappoint Your Friends, Family and Staff*

Other books by Mark Geoffrey Young

The West Australian Joke Book
How To Promote Your Business
Dr. Young's Guide to Demotivating Employees
Guide To Selling Your Home

And 750+ other books titled:

The Best Ever Book of ...... Jokes

**To find out more, check out**

**www.dolyttle.com**

**or visit**

**www.amazon.com**

# THE BEST EVER GUIDE TO DEMOTIVATION FOR HUMAN RESOURCE MANAGERS

*How To Dismay, Dishearten and Disappoint Your Friends, Family and Staff*

*By Mark Geoffrey Young*

*Illustrated by T. R. Patrick*

*Introduction by Dick DeBartolo*

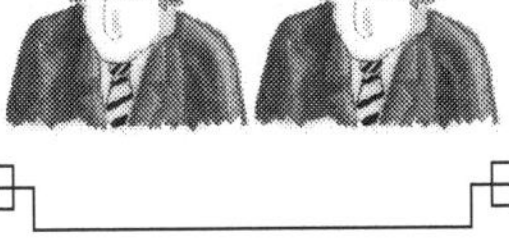

*Dolyttle & Seamore*

*New York, NY*

The Best Ever Guide to Demotivation: How To Dismay, Dishearten and Disappoint Your Friends, Family and Staff

Dolyttle & Seamore
New York





Dolyttle & Seamore
198 Garth Road Suite 2DD
Scarsdale, NY 10583

Publisher's Cataloging-in-Publication Data

The Best Ever Guide To Demotivation: *How To Dismay, Dishearten and Disappoint Your Friends, Family and Staff*

p. cm.
ISBN-13:9781484862902
ISBN-10:1484862902

10 9 8 7 6 5 4 3 2 1

Mark Geoffrey Young; illustrated by T.R. Patrick.

**This book is dedicated to everybody who has read a motivational book and said:**

***"This crap just doesn't work for me."***

vi

# FORWARD

When I got a call asking I would like to write the forward to this book, I was quite surprised. Mostly surprised because I had no idea who the author was! But then I remembered that we had shared the last pretzel at a press gathering eleven years ago. Oh, I thought, I remember now! I was told that someone famous was needed to write the forward.

The author further explained that nobody famous was willing do it, and he was now down to the contacts on the "D" list. But I was assured that there was also an "E" and an "F" list too, so I wasn't the last hope.

When I asked what writing the forward involved, the instructions were clear and concise. "You do it for free. I'm up against a deadline, so you have to do it for free and you have to do it fast.

"I basically need you to mention in **bold type** that you're **MAD Magazine's Maddest Writer** and **The Giz Wiz** on **radio** and **TV**. And that you have a Webpage that gets hundreds of thousands of downloads a month. They're not the most impressive credentials, but you're all I got for now."

Okay, so I'm thinking to myself, "This person is honest, but it sure doesn't sound very interesting. I mean why would I bother?" Before hanging up I figured I'd ask what the book was about. “Oh my book is all about demotivation. All about making people not want to do stuff.” Hmmm. I sure did not want to write the intro to this book!

Bottom line? If someone else on the E & F list can’t be suckered into writing a better forward, this is most likely what you’ll find at the front of his book!

***Dick DeBartolo***
***MAD Magazine’s Maddest Writer and The Giz Wiz***
***www.gizwiz.biz***

# DEFINITIONS

**De·mot·i·vate** *v.* The ability to inspire people to ignore a specific subject or topic and take absolutely no action in this area.

**De·mot·i·vat·ed** *adj.* Affected or marked by being unable to take action in a specific area or areas.

**De·mot·i·vat·ion** *n.* The act of inspiring people to take absolutely no action on a specific topic or topics, regardless of how hopeful the situation may appear.

**De·mot·i·va·tion·ism** *n.* The art and science of demotivation.

**De·mot·i·va·tion·al·ism** *(British variant of* **Demotivationism.** *This term is used by all members of the Commonwealth of Nations with the exception of Australia, Canada and Grenada).*

**De·mot·i·va·tion·ist** *n.* A person who inspires people to accept their menial position in society and helps them realize that they should make the most of what they have, as their situation is unlikely to change.

**De·mot·i·va·tion·al·ist** *(British variant of* **Demotivationist.** *This term is used by all members of the Commonwealth of Nations with the exception of Australia, Canada and Grenada).*

**De·mot·i·va·tion·ists** *n.* An obscure nineteenth-century cult organized by large American landowners that was devoted to discouraging enthusiasm, entrepreneurialism and vision amongst slaves, indentured workers and small-scale farmers.

*I've worked for assholes for my entire life. Now it's my turn to be the asshole.*

If you make a mistake (very unlikely because Human Resource Managers are as close to perfect as they come), and somebody notices, tell that person that you'll apologize if it will make them feel better.

When having a party at your home, advise all your guests that it's a BYO everything party. You'll save a fortune on food, and you'll end up making a profit because most of your friends will leave all they stuff they bought behind.

Prevent your salespeople from working too hard by taking away their existing accounts when they get too many clients. They'll appreciate the fact that you're looking after their interests.

Maintain your office hierarchy and prevent your staff from mixing with your customers by only allowing the workers to enter and exit your premises through the rear doors. While this may appear overly harsh, you need to take steps to establish your superiority as a Human Resource Manager.

If you're looking for new workers and several applicants meet your requirements, show them how good a Human Resource Manager you are by holding a reverse auction for the position. By getting them to bid against each other for the position, you'll not only save money by choosing the cheapest worker, your other employees will also see how easy they are to replace.

Reduce disruptions during the workday by scheduling all meetings for 5:00 p.m. Friday. This makes it easy for your employees to use the weekend to get a head start on next week's work.

As a Human Resource Manager, you're extremely aware that your company's cash flow will vary due to a number of different factors. Share this pain with your employees by letting their payroll checks bounce when things get a little bit tight.

When your workers are sent on a business trip, let them know that they're still expected to work their normal business hours—and remain contactable—regardless of what time it is in the city they're visiting.

Let everybody know that you operate on "Human Resource Manager time" by always showing up thirty minutes late for meetings. Never apologize for being late: it sets a bad precedent for the future.

Human Resource Managers are very good at reducing costs when it comes to children. Since most people don't keep track of how often parents volunteer to drive the group, you can save a fortune and get some extra time for yourself if you're never available. Since the kids do have to be picked up, someone will always cover for you and ensure that your child gets home.

Cut the amount of toilet paper, towels and soap you have to buy by training a camera on every dispenser in your company's bathroom. Fine those workers who exceed their allocation—or call the police and have them charged with stealing your property.

Recognize your workers by holding an employee appreciation day every year to thank them for everything

*When filling an open position, never ask existing workers or family members about the skills needed for that job. This is especially true if you have no expertise in that area.*

they've done. Charge a small—but realistic—entry price to gain access to this after-hours function.

Let your workers know how valuable "Human Resource Manager time" is by making them wait at least twenty minutes to see you—even when they have an appointment.

Show your friends and employees that Human

Resource Managers can relate to the common people by complaining about how lazy your butler, chauffeur, nanny, pilot and landscape architect are.

Place your children and other relatives in charge of as many divisions in your organization as possible—regardless of their age or qualifications. Not only will you reduce your costs, you'll also get the lowdown on everything that's happening.

Keep salary increases to a minimum by turning your skilled workers into your assistants. When it comes to review time, you can honestly point out that they're not doing the jobs you hired them to do.

Show everybody that you're a smart Human Resource Manager by charging sales tax to all your customers—even those who live out of state. If a customer complains, blame a worker and promise to refund the overcharged amount. Most clients will never check their statements to see if you followed through.

Smart Human Resource Managers everywhere are reducing their operating costs by deducting a couple of dollars from their workers' paychecks each week to cover the cost of the water and other supplies that they use in the bathroom.

If your company sells retail products, show how great a Human Resource Manager you are by offering your friends and relatives a discount. They'll never know how small the discount is—or how much money you're making from them—unless you tell them.

When one of your friends or relatives makes a mistake, no matter how minor, chastise him or her in front of everybody. Not only will you show how smart Human Resource Managers are, you'll increase their knowledge on this subject. Most people—if they're true friends—will thank you for setting them right.

Show everybody that you're an organized Human Resource Manager by always having weekly meeting—even when there's absolutely nothing to discuss.

If you ever hear laughter or talking coming from a cubicle or hallway, rush out and berate your workers. Tell them that you run a workplace—not a comedy club—and if they've run out of things to do, you have additional work available.

Make everybody more productive by refusing to share information with them at work and home. This forces them to develop their own research skills.

Install phones in every bathroom stall and above the urinals so your employees can continue working while they do their business.

Boost your productivity as a Human Resource Manager by calling your office while you're stuck in the morning traffic. This will allow you to talk to your workers while they're still fresh, and ensures that you're fully prepared the minute you enter the building.

Give your workers extra assignments to complete while they're flying. Remind them that you're paying for their airfare, so you expect them to work. Tell them that if they want to watch the movies or dine on the airline's gourmet fare, they can pay for their own trip.

If you employ workers with foreign accents, complain loudly that you can't understand a word that they're saying. Tell them if they don't learn English, you're going to replace them. This is especially effective with Canadians, Australians and British citizens.

Nobody gets a better deal at restaurants tha Human Resource Managers. Before dividing up the bill, calculate your share and work out if it's cheaper to split the bill evenly, or for everybody to pay their own share. Do this every time to save the maximum amount possible.

Allow all of your telephone calls to go into voicemail and return them in a single session when you have a free moment. Being a constantly unavailable Human

Resource Manager, encourages all of your friends, relatives and employees to solve their own problems.

Prevent back-stabbing by removing your organization's suggestion boxes. Allowing people to make unsolicited comments encourages costly and impractical ideas.

Install suggestion boxes wherever possible. This shows that Human Resource Managers care about what the common people think. It also encourages employees or club members to put forward anonymous ideas—and allows you to take credit for every unsolicited suggestion.

Show how expensive it is to run a business by having your workers provide their own supplies such as paper, pens, soap and toilet paper.

Let your workers know how valuable they are—and show how the company can't do without them—by constantly rescheduling their vacation to a time that's more convenient for the company.

Every Human Resource Manager knows that meetings are a complete waste of time. Make yourself more efficient by turning up at every meeting fifteen minutes late, leaving early, and popping in and out while it's in progress.

If a worker makes a decision, it's you're duty as a

*Volume is the best way to get your message across. If a person has a problem understanding your needs, raising your voice ensures that you always get whatever you want.*

Human Resource Manager to question him or her thoroughly about why they've chosen that course of action. Use this opportunity to remind him or her about all of their other incorrect decisions.

Reduce your travel costs by booking your workers into independent hotels and motels. Well-known chains charge a lot more than their unbranded siblings to cover their advertising costs.

Liquor stores often unload their old wine and scotch on

unsuspecting customers. Human Resource Managers are aware of this scam, and prevent themselves from being taken advantage of by refusing to purchase any alcohol or wine that's more than twelve-months old.

Maintain the distance between yourself, the Human Resource Manager, and your friends by never smiling or saying hello to anybody. While this may appear rude, it's better than having to deal with their problems.

Don't waste time sending out newsletters, emails and texts to friends or employees. People who need information will always find it, and everyone else will thank you for not wasting their time.

As a Human Resource Manager, it's important to have friends in many different fields. The more friends you have, the less you have to pay for services, and the more stuff you can get for free.

When your friends realize how smart Human Resource Managers are, they'll call you up often for advice. Tell them that you'd love to help, but you're busy now. Most of them will forget to call you back later.

Use family members in your organization whenever possible. This not only ensures an endless supply of cheap labor, it keeps your employees on their toes by showing them how easy they are to replace.

Stop your workers from using the bathrooms as a reading room by installing a camera outside the door to see who brings bags, books and magazines into the facilities.

Revitalize friendships by constantly changing your opinions and plans without consultation—before your friends can object. Allowing them to comment on long-established traditions undermines your superiority as a Human Resource Manager.

Show how good a Human Resource Manager you are by constantly asking your friends, relatives and workers about their career. Even though you may ask the same scripted questions every time you see them, just asking shows how much you care. This will dramatically increase your popularity amongst these people.

Challenge employees with boring, meaningless jobs by deliberately placing obstacles in their way. Not only will they work harder to meet your expectations as a Human Resource Manager, they'll obtain a sense of accomplishment when they finally get to where they're going.

*Use fear to get your employees to work harder. Instead of issuing verbal threats, simply scatter a few pamphlets throughout your office mentioning the advantages of overseas outsourcing.*

Let workers know that you're watching them by installing surveillance cameras above their desks. Call the at random throughout the day to find out why they're not sitting at their designated place.

Show your friends and club members how smart Human Resource Managers are by using jargon and technical terms. Don't worry if you don't know their meaning or pronunciation—neither will anybody else.

Show your compassionate side as a Human Resource Manager by helping your friends get through their rough patches by discussing their confidential problems with them in public places.

Even the smartest Human Resource Managers know that sometimes there's absolutely no way to get around giving a worker a raise. When this occurs, increase the number of hours they're required to work by the same percentage as their raise to keep your costs under control.

When an employee goes on vacation, use the opportunity to Spring clean your offices. Since not everything you collect is garbage, place all of the items you've collected in their cubicle. Hopefully your staff will have time to go through it before the vacationing employee returns.

When the weather is nice, workers often use the opportunity to eat lunch outdoors in your parking lot or in the company gardens. Eliminate this practice immediately as it can prevent your customers from easily entering and leaving the premises.

After a worker completes a course of study, let him or her know that you expect them to spend more time working as they no longer have to waste time studying or traveling to and from school.

Remember Human Resource Managers don't have friends. The people who you hang around with have two purposes: to increase your income, and to help you get to the next level. If you're "friends" are not helping you here, find new "friends" who can help make it happen.

Let workers know that revenue is not an indication of profitability. Point out that because increased revenue means increased costs, you'll be unable to grant any bonuses or raises this year.

Send out negative emails on Friday afternoons. When workers arrive at work on Monday, it will set the week's tone. This is especially effective on holiday weekends.

Friends, relatives and employees are often afraid to ask for your input. As a Human Resource Manager, you have a moral obligation to put forward all of your ideas before anybody asks for your opinion.

Get your employees to work harder by insisting that they teach their job to one of your summer interns. If a worker misbehaves in the future, threaten to bring the intern back.

Whenever your revenues exceed expectations, your workers will feel that they're entitled to share in the rewards. Kill this conversation by reminding them that even though interns could do their jobs, you're not planning to lay anybody off.

Because workers don't have the same standards as Human Resource Managers, reserve at least one bathroom stall and sink for your exclusive use. This ensures cleanliness and prevents your workers from transmitting any contagious diseases they may be carrying.

Inform your workers that elective surgery is a self-induced illness (like a hangover) that doesn't qualify as for sick time. Tell them if they want to be paid, they must use their vacation.

Let your workers know that it's their job to make you look good as a Human Resource Manager. Remind them that if you look bad, everybody looks bad. And, if this happens, everybody will be looking for another job.

Show your friends how Human Resource Managers relate to the common people by telling funny jokes and stories about them and your other friends. People always think it's funny to hear embarrassing stories about themselves when others are present.

Motivate your workers by letting them know that not only are you a fabulous Human Resource Manager, you're also great in bed. Passing on these sort of tips not only improves their home life—it also makes you much more popular at work.

Blaming the people who fix your car or repair your air conditioning for damage is an easy way to save money. Most of these people are nowhere near as smart as Human Resource Managers, and will readily accept the fact that at least some of the damage was caused by them and reduce your bill accordingly.

Remove every second light bulb in your home or office to reduce your electricity costs. This not only cuts your power bill, it also saves you money in the long term because you only have to replace half as many bulbs when they burn out.

Because employees are not as smart as Human Resource Managers, never allow them to eat or drink during meetings as it can cause misunderstandings later. Very few workers can think and chew at the same time.

Remove a worker's nameplate from their cubicle before you let him or her go. If you leave the former employee's name on the wall, it will remind your remaining workers that this person once worked for you.

While only a Human Resource Manager can make decisions, get your lower-level employees involved in

*Reduce the stresses of business travel by allowing your workers to visit clients while they're on vacation. They'll thank you when they return for not having to waste time traveling when they return.*

this process early so you have a scapegoat to blame in the unlikely event that something goes wrong.

Let employees know how important their jobs are by telling them how you, as a Human Resource Manager, built your business without anybody's help or support. This is an especially effective motivator after they've just completed a rush job or worked through their weekend to meet a very tight deadline.

Keep your sick employees in the loop by calling them frequently while they're recovering at home. Just because they can't get into the office, doesn't mean they're incapable of working from home.

Get the news from your traveling workers quickly by forcing everybody to return to the office immediately after their flight lands. If it's a red eye or night flight, give them until 9:00 a.m. to arrive at the office.

Encourage your employees to work harder by placing a grade on every piece of work they hand in. This always inspires them to try harder as everybody wants an "A" on their report.

Let everyone know you're a compassionate Human Resource Manager by allowing an employee who received an award to speak about their most recent success for a FULL minute at a company meeting. Get them to emphasize how your support made their achievement possible.

Over time your workers may realize that their job is meaningless and lose enthusiasm. Prevent this from happening by reminding them continually that no matter how well they perform, or how hard they work, you'll never be satisfied with anything they produce.

Every time an employee makes an error, suspend them and replace them with a temp for a day or two. This shows your other employees how easy everybody is to replace.

Motivate your workers to constantly improve their writing skills by continually editing their work. Make revisions to every version—even if the document is acceptable.

Reward those workers who complete their tasks early, and have time to stand around talking, by giving them additional work to complete.

Keep your workers on their toes and prevent them from asking for a raise by sharing only bad news with them. Instead of letting your employees know when you make a large sale or acquire a new client, only provide them with news when something goes wrong or a client leaves.

When you let a worker go, simply say "you're fired" and call security. Allowing a laid-off worker to return to their desk will only cause a scene, disrupt your office's productivity and undermine your authority as a Human Resource Manager.

Get your friends and employees to go the extra mile by hiring a private investigator to uncover information about them. Threaten to reveal this to their family and friends if they ever upset you or say no when you ask them for a favor.

*Keep a close eye on every task your employees are working on and offer your input—even if you have absolutely no expertise in this area. When the job is completed, have them point out your contribution.*

Make your company more profitable by promoting from within whenever possible. Not only do you save money by not having to increase the affected worker's salary, you improve morale by giving the worker a new title.

Never promote from within unless you can't find an external candidate. Hiring an existing employee means you have to fill two vacancies—the promoted worker's position, and the open job.

Even though you may not be starting a project for some time, send out an urgent email requesting information at the first opportunity. This ensures that you receive the respect and recognition you deserve as a Human Resource Manager, as well as having everything you need to begin the task when you're ready.

Help your employees stay in shape by placing staff parking spaces as far away from your building as possible. Your workers will thank you for helping them get exercise and eliminating the need for them to hire a personal trainer.

Funerals are a time of sadness for everybody concerned. Show everybody how compassionate Human Resource Managers are by giving the affected worker time off to attend the event. Remind them that it's not an all-day occasion and that you expect them in the office before and after the event.

Ensure a good attendance at your holiday party by telling workers who choose not to attend that they're required to remain at their desks working until their normal quitting time.

Don't waste time talking about your competitors. Your workers will function much better if they only have to concern themselves with your products.

When costs need to be cut, reduce all of your workers hours. Remind any employees who choose to complain that unions of yesteryear fought for better working conditions and more time off—and they should be grateful to you for continuing this fight.

Blame every error on somebody else because Human Resource Managers don't make mistakes. If an employee claims otherwise, fire him or her. This reduces the likelihood of other workers challenging you and allows you to live a peaceful existence.

Get the home phone numbers of your workers in different time zones so you can contact them whenever needed. Having to wait until their normal business hours could dramatically reduce your productivity.

Show your staff that they're part of your team by giving everyone a nickname. Baldy, Skinny, Tiny, Shorty and Fatty are good starting points.

Never apologize to workers for the size of their bonus. Instead, point out that many employees only receive their base salary, and that you'll move to this model if they continue to complain.

Get your workers to treat the company's money like

their own by deducting all customer refunds and credits from their paychecks.

When an employee resigns, remind them how much you've done for them as a Human Resource Manager during their tenure, and let them know that you see their leaving as a personal affront.

If you leave your employees to their own devices, they'll find the easiest way to do their job and rush out the door at the first opportunity. While you may not begrudge your employees a happy home life, remember, their only purpose is to make your life easier.

Cut the salaries of your older workers when they lose their edge. When they complain, remind them that they're not as sharp as they used to be. Tell them that there are many younger workers who are prepared to do their job for less than their new, reduced salary.

Young employees often believe that they're worth a lot more than you pay them. Point out how many older, more experienced workers would happily do their job for a pittance of what you're currently paying them.

Inform employees that their vacation starts after the office closes—not twenty or thirty minutes before their normal workday ends. Prevent them from stealing your time by assigning them a last-minute project to complete before they depart.

Keep your office door closed whenever possible. Not only does this prevent interruptions, it shows your workers how important you are as a Human Resource Manager. Since nobody walks in to the President's or King's office unannounced, keeping your door shut at all times places you in the same league.

If an employee is injured or required to perform light duties for a period of time, calculate the impact this will have on their performance and reduce their salary by this percentage.

Home-based workers are more likely to take advantage of you as a Human Resource Manager than any of your other employees. Prevent this from happening by getting them to fill in on-line worksheets every fifteen minutes.

When a worker has to leave early for an emergency, say loudly "thanks for dropping in." Your employees will take advantage of your "niceness" as a Human Resource Manager if they think you're not paying attention to their hours.

To generate additional income, stock your vending machines with generic sodas and foods. While this items may be sub-par, they'll sell well because you have a monopoly on what's sold on your premises.

*Make your company more profitable by allowing charities to place donation cans in your lunchrooms and in the public areas of your business. Use these donations to reduce your taxable income.*

If your workers need to work late or on a weekend to meet a deadline, resist the urge to join them. Having a Human Resource Manager on the premises after hours could make them feel uncomfortable. Instead, call them frequently from your beach house to check on how things are going and offer moral support.

Encourage your workers to take part in community

activities on their own time and allow them to display the awards they win in your reception area. Remember, it's your generosity as a Human Resource Manager to give them weekends and nights off that makes it possible for them to win awards.

Human Resource Managers need a firm but compassionate policy to deal with tardy employees. The first time the worker is late, reduce their pay by the appropriate number of minutes—then double it for each subsequent offense.

Call and text your employees while they're on vacation a couple of times a day to keep them up to date with what's happening in the office. While this may appear intrusive, it saves time when they return to work.

When your fire a worker, never, ever tell your staff that you let an employee go. Telling your workers that an employee is no longer part of the team will only encourage them to worry about their own jobs.

Commissioned salespeople always complain about the size of their commissions. Eliminate disputes by refusing to share "raw" revenue figures with them.

When you have to leave before a normal workday ends, call your workers from the road before their scheduled departure. If they've taken advantage of your absence and left early, deduct the appropriate amount of money from their salary.

Show workers how progressive you are as a Human Resource Manager by offering everybody flexible hours and allowing them to work at home when needed. Question their loyalty if they take you up on this offer.

If you're forced to eliminate part-time jobs due to economic conditions, point out how compassionate you are as a Human Resource Manager by allowing your remaining employees to work voluntary (and unpaid) overtime to prevent further retrenchments.

As a Human Resource Manager, it's OK to share other workers' salary information when an employee asks for a raise. Instead of listening to their reasoning, simply show them how little one of their coworkers earns. This will make them realize how good they have it.

Remember all grapes grow on vines, and all wine is made from grapes. Show how smart you are as a Human Resource Manager by purchasing the cheapest wine available from your local discounter.

If there's no way to meet a client's deadline, deliver the parts of the job that you've completed. Tell your workers to blame someone else and have them inform the client that the boss is looking into it.

*Workers love stories about how things used to be done. When you have time, explain how you used to work every night and weekend—and still managed to get to work early on Mondays.*

Remind everybody that you're in charge by making every decision without input. As a Human Resource Manager, you're always right. If the facts don't match your opinions, change your mind and claim that was always your viewpoint.

Challenge your friends, relatives and employees to reach for the stars by getting them set their goals so high that they can never be reached. To reinforce you superiority as a Human Resource Manager, remind everybody how you managed to reach your goals.

If you're forced to close early due to a power failure, unfavorable weather conditions or an emergency, give your workers the opportunity to make up the lost hours by working late the following day. If this can't be done, dock their pay the appropriate amount.

Ensure that everybody meets your standards by signing off on everything—no matter how menial it may appear—while simultaneously complaining about how busy you are as a Human Resource Manager. Delegating tasks always causes problems.

Have your workers teach your children how to do their jobs. Tell them that while their positions are secure for the moment, you do intend to pass the business on to your children eventually. As a result, it's essential that your children know what everybody does—and how they do it—even if they haven't yet graduated from elementary school.

Show your workers how much you value their services, and reinforce how important they are, by placing them on call for the weekends that fall on both sides of their vacation.

Titles are great motivators. Keep your employees working hard by allocating—and reallocating—titles, based on their contribution to your company in a particular month.

Most workers regard overtime as voluntary and expect to be paid for it. Dispel this myth by taking everybody off the clock and classifying them as "exempt" employees who are not entitled to overtime.

Don't introduce new workers, club members or friends to each other as it encourages gossip. Keeping things on a professional level ensures that everyone knows their place in your mind.

Make friends with your workers by walking around the office and saying "good morning" to everybody at 9:00 a.m. every day, and again at 5:00 p.m. in the evening. Not only does this show how approachable you are as a Human Resource Manager, it lets you see who made it to work on time and who left early. You can then penalize those workers take advantage of you.

Encourage your workers to increase their knowledge of your industry by sending them to seminars and trade shows during their vacation. Make it cost-effective for the employee by offering to split the cost of one night's hotel accommodation with them.

Prevent your clients and friends from stealing your staff and corrupting their minds by refusing them access to your facilities.

Make your employees work harder by refusing to hire temporary workers during peak periods. If an employee complains, remind him or her that their predecessors were able to do their job without help.

Ensure that your workers learn from their mistakes by pointing out every error, no matter how small, in front of clients. Then apologize to the customer for not having employees who are up to the task.

Make your staff feel good by asking for their opinions before you leave the meeting. Because you're leaving, have them email their comments to you so you can give them the consideration they deserve.

Instead of offering workers bonuses, salary increases or praise when they do more than is expected of them, let employees know that you expect this sort of sustained effort on a regular basis.

Generate extra income by hiring workers who speak other languages so you can expand your business into new communities. To encourage a feeling of belonging, insist that all employee communications on your premises take place in English.

No matter how good you think your employees are, or

how hard they appear to work, the sad fact of the matter is that no worker is as good as a Human Resource Manager. Every worker will take advantage of you if you give them the opportunity. Prevent this from happening by constantly pushing them in the right direction—even when things are working perfectly.

If a worker is unhappy with their bonus or salary, suggest that they take it up with their Congressman. Point out that if you didn't have to pay taxes on your revenue, you'd have more money to share with every worker who is beneath you.

Never allow employees to set their own hours. Instead set "core" hours, say 8:00 a.m. to 5:00 p.m., when everybody is required to be at work. Allow workers to spend additional time in the office when necessary.

Show how progressive Human Resource Managers are by instituting a casual dress code. Let them know that they're being watched by commenting frequently about the clothes they're wearing.

If one of your children fails to achieve his or her potential, get one of your workers with expertise in that subject area to voluntarily tutor them after work. Base this worker's bonus on how well your child does.

Show your workers how Human Resource Managers can make everybody more efficient and reduce the amount

*Recognize employees who perform well by giving them additional work. This not only shows how pleased you are with a worker's performance, it lets you replace higher-paid employees with lower-paid workers.*

of time employees waste by following your staff into the bathroom and asking them questions as they do their business.

Spend a lot of time with your employees discussing how every change will affect your organization. Look at every minute detail, regardless of how small it appears, to ensure that you're fully prepared.

If there's no way to avoid praising a worker, do it through a third-party. If you do something once it becomes company policy and you'll be forced to do it again and again.

When you see an employee working on a project that they're enjoying, reassign it immediately to another worker. If your employees are having fun and enjoying their jobs, they're not working.

Keep your workers on the ball by tossing paper clips and other items at them as you pass their desk. This is especially effective with employees who appear to have had a hard night or who are recovering from an illness.

Keep your employees on their toes by running ads for every position in your company at least twice a year. This makes it easy for you to replace inefficient workers—and encourages everybody to work harder.

Whenever you have a bad day or something goes wrong, call the nearest worker into your office and berate them. Employees need to know how tough it is being a Human Resource Manager—and when to approach you.

Booking last minute vacations is both difficult and expensive. Give your workers plenty of notice by posting the vacation schedule in January. Show how flexible you are by allowing them to make changes with six months notice.

Increase the size of your donations by allowing charities to use your premises for their meetings rent-free. This allows you to claim the rent you didn't receive as a tax deduction.

Let your employees know that Human Resource Managers are superior to everybody by refusing to help clean up or carry equipment to distant locations. Feel free to continually complain about how much you're paying your workers or how slowly they're working.

When employees work overtime or come in on a weekend, remind them that they're professionals and that you expect them to do whatever it takes to get their job done.

When a worker must be praised, do it in private without any witnesses. This will prevent your words being used against you in future salary negotiations.

Improve your productivity by eliminating the need for your workers to think. By over-specifying everything you want done, you allow your workers to spend their time doing their job, instead of thinking about it.

Give your workers a feeling of ownership by encouraging them to find the best way to do their jobs. Offering guidance and suggestions turns your skilled employees

*Deduct a security deposit from an employee's first paycheck to cover their company ID, keys, uniforms and other property. Return this upon termination if everything is returned in its original, pristine condition.*

into mere assistants.

Have your workers to raise their hand or ring a bell when they need to use the bathroom. Knowing that they're being monitored dramatically reduces the amount of time they need to use the facilities.

Encourage your workers to expand their horizons by assigning them tasks that are outside their area of expertise. Allowing employees to acquire new skills and expertise ensures that everybody benefits.

Never allow workers to set their own deadlines or tell you how long a job will take to complete. Letting employees set their own targets and deadlines shows that you're a weak Human Resource Manager and this will cause them to question your authority.

To encourage learning, get your employees to print out all their documents and walk them over to you for review. Making your comments directly onto their printouts ensures that your workers learn from their mistakes by forcing them to input your changes manually.

Since status is very important to workers, hand out fancy titles when you conduct salary reviews. Your employees will respect you as a Human Resource Manager and appreciate the fact that you've given them something to brag about with their friends over dinner.

Because many factors can determine how many workers are needed on a weekend, decide which employees will work at 4:30 p.m. on Friday. Staff who are not needed will appreciate the time off.

Provide only instant coffee to your workers. If your employees complain, remind them that they're free to purchase their own gourmet coffee, decaf, hot chocolate or tea if they don't like the beverages you provide.

Bond with your workers and let them know that Human Resource Managers have a sense of humor by offering to share your jokes with them as soon as the workday is over.

Insist that workers keep the windows closed when the air conditioning fails to reduce the chance of bugs getting into your computers.

Let your workers know that researching work projects on the Internet should be conducted on their own time.

Just because a worker does a great job doesn't mean he or she is entitled to a raise or a bonus. Instead of increasing their pay, remind them that there's more to a job than just a paycheck.

No matter how much time you spend training your workers, or how specific your instructions are, your employees are going to screw up and upset your customers. When this happens question whether they were paying attention during the training session—regardless of how long ago it took place.

Inspire creativity in your workers by refusing to issue credits or refunds to your valued customers. They'll enjoy the challenge of appeasing unhappy customers

*When you're on vacation, let your workers know that you're always available on your cell phone. If you don't get back to them before the decision needs to be made, berate them for making the wrong choice.*

when they can't take the easy and obvious route to client satisfaction.

Support your local high schools and colleges by letting their students work as interns during your busy periods. As well as reducing your labor costs, you'll help the students get real-world training that will make it easier for them to find a job when they graduate.

Instead of seating your workers in the department where they work, organize seating based on attractiveness.

Placing your beautiful staff members in the front where your clients can see them creates a better first impression. Rearrange the seating every time you hire or fire an employee.

Give every worker a target and quota that's impossible to reach and chastise those who fail to hit that number. If you make your targets achievable, your workers will realize you're a weak Human Resource Manager and cease working the moment they hit their goal.

Stop your employees from leaving early by walking through the halls every day between 4:30 p.m. and 5:30 p.m. While this may appear to be a waste of your time, it's more productive than allowing your workers to leave before their day actually ends.

Build your company spirit and recognize those workers who do what's required by getting everybody to compete for a single bonus called a "reward."

Reduce your costs by eliminating disposable cups and napkins in the kitchen and insisting that workers provide their own coffee cups. If an employee has a visitor, they can bring an extra cup from home or borrow one from a coworker.

Charge workers who visit friends or relatives while traveling on business a portion of the trip's cost. After all, it's only fair that they pay their share if they turn a work trip into a vacation.

Insist that people who can't physically be at a meeting, attend by phone—regardless of where they happen to be at the time. This also applies to employees on vacation and those who live in other countries.

When an employee gets a difficult issue under control, show your appreciation as a Human Resource Manager by reallocating this task to another employee and moving them to an area that makes better use of their skills.

Help your workers learn how valuable their time is by forcing them to resolve all customer complaints in less than three minutes. Penalize employees for every interaction that exceeds this time.

Cash in on the fact that tall people are more credible by insisting that all of your employees wear six-inch platform shoes. You'll also reduce the number of complaints you receive, because customers will be afraid to argue with people who appear to be tall.

Make your company seem bigger than it is by creating an impressive front lobby and waiting room for your clients. Your staff will happily put up with cramped conditions if they know your customers are happy.

*When friends visit your home, remind them to bring their own soap and toilet paper. This saves money because you don't have to share your supplies, and increases your cash flow as many people will forget to take their supplies home with them.*

Reduce the pressure that vacationing workers place on their coworkers by only allowing your employees to take a maximum of one week's vacation at any time—regardless of their circumstances. You, as a Human Resource Manager, are of course exempt from this policy.

Show respect for your customers by refusing to allow your staff to use the customer facilities—or your customers to use the staff facilities—even when their bathrooms are out of order.

Maintain your company spirit by insisting that your workers to sign an agreement stating that anything they invent, write or develop after they start working for you—belongs to you—even if they come up with the idea after work or long after they leave your company.

Encourage a feeling of belonging by getting your workers to contribute to the cost of beverages by forming an office coffee club. Show how liberal you are as a Human Resource Manager by inviting everybody to join—regardless of their status in your company.

Show how smart Human Resource Managers are by making small donations to as many community organizations as possible. This will allow you to use their logos on your stationery and signage. If you choose the right organizations, their members will patronize your company and the increased business will more than pay for your tax-deductible donations.

Forward all your calls to voicemail. To show your customers how important Human Resource Managers are, get your workers to call them back. Anybody who really wants to speak to you directly will call again.

Prevent your workers from resting on their laurels when they break a production record. Instead of praising them for doing a great job, complain loudly that if they were able to once, they should be able to do it every time.

Have your staff generate extra income by billing clients for any extra services they use while visiting your office. This includes using your paper, pens, phones and drinking your coffee or water.

Since most of your clients can't add, make their life easier by having your cash registers and accounting programs automatically round up all your prices to the nearest dollar. Apologize and blame your workers if a customer complains.

Prevent employees from abusing your Internet connection by monitoring usage. At the end of each week, produce a log and get them to justify every site they visited.

Show how tough you are as a Human Resource Manager and stop your bar employees from giving away your profits by measuring how much alcohol is on the premises when they start their shift—and how much is left when they finish. Deduct discrepancies from their salary.

Even though telephone calls are cheaper than ever, you still have to pay for them. A simple way to reduce your costs is to get two or three workers to share a single phone line.

Keep your reputation as a Human Resource Manager intact by getting your workers to call a customer when you miss a deadline. Using the excuse that it's better to get something right and late, than to get it wrong and on time, will always make your customer feel better.

Prevent your restaurant workers from giving away too-large portions by calculating exactly how many people you can feed with the food you purchased. Charge your employees if the food you bought doesn't stretch as far as you expect it to.

Motivate your workers to sell more by telling them that unless they sell $10,000 worth of goods in the next four hours, you're going to close down the company. Do this often for maximum effect.

Encourage your employees to use public transportation and conserve gas by charging them a fee to use your staff parking lot.

If a worker breaks or damages something that belongs to your company, deduct the item's full retail cost from their next paycheck, regardless of how old it is. After all, you did have to buy it once.

If an employee comes up with a great idea, avoid

implementing it for as long as possible. Making changes on-the-fly causes problems because your workers are used to doing things a certain way.

Teach your workers the value of a dollar and increase your profits by charging them the full cost of their health, disability and unemployment insurance. While you may want to be a benevolent Human Resource Manager, remember, workers don't appreciate things unless they're forced to pay for them themselves.

Reduce costs, conserve paper and do your part as a Human Resource Manager to save the environment by using six-point type for all employee contracts and all other documents that have very little value.

Never share customer compliments with your employees. Letting your workers know that they're doing something right undermines your credibility as a Human Resource Manager, takes the pressure off, and encourages your employees to take it easy.

Reduce costs by refusing to order supplies until you're completely out. Employees have their own unique ways of coping during shortages, including bringing in their own equipment from home.

Help out your lower-paid workers by selling them any leftover food items from your business events at cost. Your employees will save money and you'll reduce your

*Caterers make their money by over-estimating how much food every worker will eat. Keep your costs under control by reducing the number of people expected at your function by one-third when placing the order.*

overhead.

Get your staff to work harder by hiring everybody on a temporary basis when they start. Tell them you'll make them permanent as soon as they prove their worth—regardless of how long this takes.

Let workers know that you're monitoring them by holding quarterly reviews with them and their supervisor. Use this opportunity to fault both employees for failing to live up to your expectations as a Human Resource Manager.

Reduce your stress levels by delegating often. Allowing your workers to handle mundane tasks ensures that you make the best possible use of your time—and gives you someone to blame if things go wrong..

As well as reducing productivity and creating isolation, private offices increase your costs by forcing you to rent more space than needed. The easy way to increase productivity, improve worker satisfaction and reduce your costs is to replace private offices with cubicles.

Discourage unqualified workers from applying for jobs in your company by charging them a fee to cover fingerprinting and background checks—regardless of whether you conduct these checks or not.

Whenever an employee comes up with an idea at a meeting, use your skills as a Human Resource Manager to go into great detail about why it won't work and why it's not worthy of consideration.

Even if you remember a worker's name, never use it. "Hey you," should be sufficient. To maximise your efficiency as a Human Resource Manager, you need to distinguish yourself from the workers.

Prevent your traveling workers from feeling lonely by having them share a room. Most hotels offer cots, so you can double or triple their fun and reduce your costs at the same time.

To see if a new worker has what it takes to survive in your company, wait at least six months after he or she starts to order costly supplies such as business cards.

Follow the law to the letter by never giving workers more than is required. Offering time off and bonuses causes friction and leads to a feeling of entitlement.

Reduce your phone costs by placing a jar next to each telephone. Making it easy for your workers to pay for their personal calls—and playing with their conscience—will dramatically increase your ancillary income.

Have new workers arrive thirty minutes early on their first day. Spending time in the lobby watching their coworkers arrive makes it easier for them to integrate.

Boost your profits and get your salespeople to choose their clients carefully by deducting any unpaid invoices from their salaries.

Avoid problem-solving meetings, as these events always

*Remind your staff that you're the boss by leaving the remains of your lunch in the break room when you've finished eating. Complain frequently about how messy the office is.*

become a venue for people to vent their frustrations and fail to recognize your superiority as a Human Resource Manager.

Open communication is essential is you're going to use your skills as a Human Resource Manager to the maximum. Encourage creativity by saying whatever you want, whenever you want—regardless of whose feelings you may hurt.

Small incentives are a great way to motivate your workers. Allow employees who do their job well to choose their own pens from the samples you received at your last trade show.

When workers complain about their salary, let them know that you have no objection to them getting a second or third job—as long as it doesn't interfere with their responsibilities.

Teach workers the value of the Earth's finite resources by fining employees who leave the lights on when they leave the room, or allow heat or air conditioning to escape through an open door or window.

Reward your workers for a job well done by presenting them with discount certificates for other businesses in your area. Not only will many firms give you the certificates for free, they'll thank you for driving extra business their way.

Encourage your workers to undertake both short courses and advanced degrees in their spare time. Let them know that while you're unable to contribute to the cost, it will be noted on their permanent record.

Let employees know that they're free to use the bathrooms during their breaks and before and after work. Enforce this policy by keeping the facilities locked at all other times.

Hire a temp and get him or her to learn everybody's job. This not only allows workers see their true value—it show them how easy they are to replace.

Prevent your clients and other workers from suffering when an employee takes a vacation by ensuring that everybody has the vacationing worker's cell phone number. If your employee objects, remind him or her that it only takes a few minutes to answer their phone or respond to a text.

Don't waste time explaining how your changes will impact your workers' jobs. Letting your employees know what you're planning will cost you money as they'll waste time complaining about the impact to their coworkers.

Soften up your workers for the worst by sending out newsletters in November and December highlighting the year's mistakes. This will cut your costs by reducing their expectations for bonuses and raises.

Reduce costs by encouraging your workers to come up with money-saving ideas. Show your appreciation by selling them merchandise with the company logo at slightly above cost.

Although family sizes are shrinking, workers seem to

have more relatives than ever. Prevent your employees from "inventing" family and taking unnecessary personal days by demanding a notarized death certificate when they claim they're attending a funeral.

Prevent your over-ambitious employees from getting big heads by transferring them to another job just before they complete a project. This keeps their egos under control and reduces the amount of money you have to pay out in bonuses, and ensures that you receive the respect you think you deserve as a Human Resource Manager.

Remember that everything in the company belongs to you. As such, don't feel obliged to return pens or other items that you "borrow" from your workers.

To reduce conflicts and prevent future arguments, never hire a person who appears to be more intelligent than you are as a Human Resource Manager. If they were smarter than you, you'd be joining their organization, not the other way around.

Prevent your employees from waiting on line to use the bathroom by having them email their supervisor when they need to use the facilities. When the supervisor has a moment, he or she will let the worker know that it's OK to use the facilities.

Reduce the temptation for your employees to goof

off and improve their productivity by eliminating all distractions. Blacking out all of the windows in your office is a clever idea that only a Human Resource Manager could come up with.

Whenever a worker claims that their bus or train was delayed, demand proof in the form of a notarized letter from the transport authority.

Do payroll and expense reimbursement when you have time. If someone is unhappy with the four to six week wait for their money, they're never going to fit in with the culture you're trying to build as a Human Resource Manager.

When workers complain about unrealistic deadlines, let them know if they can't meet them, you'll hire a Human Resource Manager like yourself who can.

Complain loudly to your workers that they're not doing their jobs if the competition comes up with an idea before you do. Fire the responsible party to encourage your remaining staff to keep on eye on your competitors in the future.

Remind staff that your clients are the reason your company exists. Endorse their products with unprecedented zeal—regardless of their quality, price or usefulness.

*Never get involved in your workers' personal lives. Remind them that while you would love to support their fundraisers, you're unable to due to the possibility that harassment charges could be levied against you.*

Prevent workers from taking advantage of you by disregarding their estimates of how long a project will take to complete. Instead, impose your own schedule using "Human Resource Manager time" as employees always add extra time to a project to reduce their stress levels.

If a worker has a clean desk, assign him or her additional work as they're not working to capacity. If they have time to clean their desk, they have time to complete additional tasks.

Berate workers with messy desks—it's an indication that they don't care about the image they're projecting. Let them know that good workers think nothing of spending a few extra minutes after work is over to clean up after themselves.

Allocate employee parking spaces based on a worker's value to the firm. Reallocate these spaces daily to prevent workers from becoming complacent.

Make travel fun for your traveling workers by getting them to stay just outside the city limits. They'll not only feel good about saving you a few dollars, they'll get to see an area of the city that few tourists visit.

Improve your productivity by requiring workers to clock out whenever they take a cigarette break. Not only will they spend longer at their desks if they know they're being monitored, they'll thank you for reducing their cigarette bill and improving their overall health.

When a customer brings back an item that you can't return to the manufacturer, get a worker to shrink wrap it and place it back on the shelf. The chances of it coming back a second time are very small.

Whenever a worker speaks with you, question him or her thoroughly about their motives. After all, not everybody is qualified to talk to a Human Resource Manager.

Regardless of how long a worker has been with you, how much they've contributed to the company, or why you're letting them go, never offer the departing employee a severance package. Doing so gives the worker an inflated view of their true value.

Give your long-serving workers autonomy by allowing them to make small, insignificant decisions. This helps them to feel like they're part of your team and makes their jobs seem more interesting.

When editing a document, make your corrections in purple, green or yellow pen so they stand out. Prevent your workers from getting hurt by writing your comments very small, so they don't think that you're yelling at them.

Employees have a lot of clothes they never wear. Encourage them to show them off these items by keeping the temperature at 50 degrees during winter and at 95 degrees in summer. Your employees may even decide to implement this idea at home.

Issue every worker with a defined job contract and berate those workers who take on additional responsibilities. Your other employees will be offended if someone else attempts to do their job.

*Use your company meetings to improve morale. Instead of using the time to look at the big picture, concentrate on the small, insignificant issues that really upset your workers.*

Show a genuine interest in your workers by asking about their families. Don't feel bad if you need to leave midway through a sentence—just asking shows that you care—and proves that Human Resource Managers are genuine, lovable human beings.

Having a knowledgeable workforce is essential if you're going to compete in today's marketplace. Test your employees frequently on current events and industry happenings to ensure that they're on the ball.

Let your vacationing employees know that even though they're not in the office, they're still being paid. Remind them that they must respond to texts, emails and voicemails at least twice a day.

To keep morale in your company high, never confront a worker who does something wrong. Instead, discuss the problem with your other employees to ensure that the message gets back to him or her.

Show your workers how much you value their services by using paper nameplates on offices and cubicles.

When interviewing a potential worker or club member, assert your superiority as a Human Resource Manager by refusing to shake his or her hand. This also reduces your risk of getting sick.

If a product is out of stock, get your workers to tell the customer that it's in short supply, but you do have a limited quantity arriving tomorrow. Getting a non-refundable deposit improves your cash flow and allows you to earn interest on your client's money while you wait for the item to arrive.

Complain constantly that your employees are not putting in enough hours and that you're going broke—

regardless of how many hours they're actually working.

Let your employees know that your office is only to be used for work by refusing to allow any onsite activities such as yoga to take place during their lunch break.

Create a spreadsheet that lets you record how many times each employee visits the bathroom and how long they spend using the facilities. Penalize those employees who waste too much time.

If one of your workers is sailing along without any problems, drop by their desk to find out what they're hiding from you. As a Human Resource Manager, you know too well that if an employee thinks that they can get something past you, he or she will.

Encourage your workers to come up with creative and innovative ways to do their jobs. Setting clear expectations, targets and goals costs you money as your employees will do things they way they've always been done.

Insist that your workers submit all reimbursement requests within seven days of incurring the expense. Refusing to accept expense reports outside this period will dramatically improve your cash flow.

Remember that even your most experienced workers

do not have the skills or intelligence of even an average Human Resource Manager. To encourage them to learn, look over their shoulders as you pass their desk and offer creative input to help them get it right.

Get your workers' families involved with your company by holding frequent "Bring Your Children To Work Days." Let the children know that you expect them to show their gratitude by performing worthwhile tasks such as stuffing envelopes, preparing presentations and running errands.

Stop your workers from waiting until the last minute to complete their tasks by responding to urgent emails on "Human Resource Manager Time." This will ensure they allow enough time for your input—should you decide to offer it.

Make your executives more efficient and reduce the time they have to wait to use the bathrooms by getting your employees to line up outside until your managers are finished. This also establishes an office hierarchy and reduces conflicts.

Every time a worker enters your office, let them know how important you are as a Human Resource Manager by constantly checking your emails, texts, voicemail and other tasks while they talk to you.

Make your meetings more effective by insisting that

everyone turns up on time by starting the meeting when it's scheduled. Allow latecomers to listen to the proceedings on the intercom.

Keep your bug and rodent population down by instituting a policy that prohibits workers from eating or drinking at their desks. If you close the break room at the same time, you should be able to eliminate virtually all time wasting.

Encourage your new workers to become independent by refusing to show them where the bathrooms, conference rooms and supplies are located. Industrious people will quickly locate everything they need.

Keep your company's reputation intact by insisting that every piece of work cross your desk before it's sent to a client. Call workers frequently to question their methodology and prevent mistakes.

If a worker claims that one of your ideas you developed as a Human Resource Manager won't work, get them to put all their objections in writing to prevent the meeting from getting bogged down in details.

Feel free to smoke or eat whenever you work closely with an employee. Remember, you're exempt from the normal rules of etiquette, and that the government's smoking regulations don't apply to you because you're a Human Resource Manager.

*Prevent your salespeople from earning too much money by increasing their quota every time they reach their target. Berate them the following month if they don't hit their new numbers.*

As much as you may dislike parties, they're an unfortunate part of modern-day office culture. To reduce the amount of time your employees waste, hold all functions after working hours.

Keep your employees' egos in check by constantly asking them questions about their outside interests. If a worker wins an award, ask him or her if they had a relative on the panel, or if they dated one of the judges.

Good salespeople often earn more money that their bosses who don't receive commissions. Prevent this from happening by capping the amount of money every employee in your organization can earn.

Show your generosity as a Human Resource Manager and gain worker acceptance by charging under market prices if your employees want to rent your premises to hold their annual holiday party or other function.

Support your local college and help train the next generation of leaders by getting their hospitality students to cater your office functions.

Employees often lose their inhibitions at holiday parties. Encourage them to talk about their coworkers by providing them with plenty of alcohol. Collect and store this information.

Show your staff that you're a smart Human Resource Manager by keeping an eye on everything. Use your company meetings to bring up mistakes, criticize workers and determine appropriate punishments.

Save money by giving your employees estimated starting and finishing times. This will give you the flexibility needed to alter a worker's the schedule when conditions change. Adjust their pay accordingly.

Because all good ideas come from Human Resource Managers, never ask employees for ideas. If by chance you do get a good suggestion from a worker, pass it off as your own.

Most workers feel undervalued. Prevent this from happening by running everything that concerns your business by them. This improves morale and shifts the blame off you as a Human Resource Manager, to everybody who knew about the situation.

Forbid your employees from asking your customers for input about your products and services. Giving clients the opportunity to express their opinions is asking for trouble. As a Human Resource Manager, you already know that if your customers weren't satisfied, they'd go elsewhere.

Encourage your workers to follow the law by making them responsible for any workplace violations or fines that occur on their shift.

Whenever you feel a worker is going to ask for a raise, inspire him or her to work harder by praising a former employee. Talk about their predecessor's work ethic, loyalty and his or her ability to make the impossible happen instantly.

*Keep yourself in the loop by practicing management by walking around. Not only will you catch mistakes before they occur, you'll be able to make your workers more efficient by constantly looking over their shoulders.*

Don't waste time explaining how your changes will impact your workers' jobs. Letting your employees know what you're planning will cost you money as they'll waste time complaining about the impact on their jobs to their coworkers.

Prevent workers from wasting time by turning the break room into an office and making everybody eat their lunch at their desks. This method is even more efficient if you employ hall monitors to prevent unnecessary conversation during breaks.

Reduce your costs by eliminating a worker's cell phone and email account a few days before you actually fire him or her.

Charge employees who lose or damage their company ID, keys or other property the full replacement cost, as well as an administrative fee, so they'll be more careful in the future.

Show your staff how valuable they are and recognize their achievements by holding dinners to reward those who help increase your profits. Get your employees to hold a collection to cover the costs.

To save money, workers often bring their lunch to work and store their food in your refrigerator, toast their bread in your toaster and use your microwave to heat up their soup. Reduce your electricity costs by eliminating every device that doesn't have a clearly defined business application.

Ensure all your workers are on an equal footing at your meetings and show how smart Human Resource Managers are by arranging seating alphabetically—regardless of the shape of the room or who needs to speak.

Improve communication within your company by leaving constructive voicemails on your workers' phones after they've left for the day. Feel free to raise your voice and display your emotions so they'll know exactly how you feel.

Keep your workers on their toes by sharing every piece of negative customer feedback that comes into your organization. Let your employees know that if things don't improve, you'll be forced to fire everybody.

Improve your profitability and make your company more efficient by giving every employee a set number of minutes to use the bathroom each day. Fine those who exceed their allocation.

Reward your workers by giving them discounts to the local dental, medical, hair and beauty schools. Most organizations will provide these free upon request. As well as helping your staff to look and feel great, you'll feel good knowing that you're helping to train the next generation of leaders.

Show how much Human Resource Managers care about the common people by giving the person who chairs a meeting the respect he or she deserves by demanding that everybody address them as Mr. or Ms. Chairperson.

Issue new workers and club members with your standard fifteen-page contract after they join your organization. Don't worry if it seems overly complex—

people expect these agreements be set in six-point type and written in legalese.

Allow workers to buy additional vacation time during slow periods. Charge them a fifty percent premium on their normal salary to compensate for the additional stresses their absence places on your other employees.

Reduce your unemployment costs by challenging every worker's unemployment benefits—even if you're wrong. When your ex-employees see that you're playing hardball, they'll get another job.

Hold brainstorming meetings frequently and let everybody know your true feelings as a Human Resource Manager by looking supremely bored. Feel free to complain about your workers lack of creativity.

Never compliment a worker, because the minute you do is the minute they take their job for granted and stop respecting you as a Human Resource Manager. Instead of offering praise, turn the situation around and find a fault—no matter how small—with at least one aspect of what they've done.

Since locating employees is sometimes difficult, don't hesitate to catch them just before they enter the bathroom. Because your workers know how valuable your time is as a Human Resource Manager, they'll spend as long as necessary discussing whatever is on your mind before using the facilities.

Designate a parking space near the door for the Employee of the Month. Make the worker feel loved by getting him or her to run special errands for you.

Keep your meetings short by only allowing workers to speak for one minute during meetings—regardless of the topic, their expertise, or how many employees are present. Of course, you as a Human Resource Manager, are exempt from this rule.

Make life easy on your cleaning staff by holding your holiday party at a worker's house. Compensate this worker by giving him or her the afternoon off on half pay to prepare for the event.

Inform your traveling workers that you still expect them to complete their normal work while they're visiting clients in another city. After all, every hotel room comes with a bed that they can rest their computer on.

When a worker finally gets a degree or qualification, keep his or her ego in check by explaining that you expect them to make fewer mistakes now that they're educated.

When you need to shock an employee, tell him or her that their performance is sub-par and that you're going

*When you can't find anything wrong with an employee's work, just state that you're not happy with it. This keeps him or her on their toes and forces them to worker harder.*

to let them go in 45 days if they don't improve. Never mention this conversation again.

Prevent workers from goofing off when they're traveling by issuing them time sheets to detail their activities. This will let you see exactly how much time they spend working.

When a piece of equipment breaks, replace it with a device that's older than the one that failed. This encourages workers to respect your company's property.

Improve productivity by insisting that your workers remove their jackets and coats before they enter the office. Having everyone ready to work the minute they reach their desks, dramatically reduces the amount of time your employees can steal from you.

Meetings are the perfect opportunity for your to catch up on stuff. Use your smart phone to the max—your club members, family and employees will fill you in if you miss something.

Get your workers to share your cash flow problems by paying expenses on the 30th of the month after they're submitted.

If revenues fall, inform your employees that it's because they're not working as hard as you do as a Human Resource Manager. Let them know that if their attitudes don't improve, you'll be forced to lay off workers.

Get workers to pay for their own meals when they're traveling. Remind them that since they have to eat at home, their meals are not your responsibility.

When a worker is given an award for volunteering, issue a press release so the whole town can see how you as a Human Resource Manager encourage your workers to play an active role in their local community.

Regardless of how small your town is, there are always organizations looking for help. Make it easy for your workers to donate by pre-screening these non-profits and circulating donation sheets for those charities that your Human Resource Manager friends support.

Get the most out of your workers by allocating each of them a specific time to use the facilities. If they complain, remind them how they managed to do their business between classes when they were students.

Get your workers involved with your family by allowing them to baby-sit your children on nights and weekends. Tell them you won't be offended if they bring along some work to complete after your kids fall asleep.

After a worker starts giving you the information you requested—scream at the top of your voice that you're a busy Human Resource Manager and that you only want the headline, not the feature story.

Eliminate the need for your employees to leave the premises to buy food during work hours by installing vending machines on your premises. Charge the machine owner a fee to cover electricity and rent, as well as a commission on every item sold.

*Encourage your workers to multi-task by having them work on several projects simultaneously—each with a different boss. This helps them obtain skills in different areas, and gives them feedback from several managers.*

Instead of promoting workers, give them an acting title. You'll save money, and the employee will get the experience they need to advance their career. It's a win-win situation for everybody.

Only let senior management speak at company meetings—and only on topics that you find relevant. Allowing every employee to participate is a sure-fire recipe for chaos.

Improve the overall cleanliness of your bathroom by getting your workers to take turns cleaning them on their own time. Because your employees are the ones who use the facilities, they'll take extra care to ensure that they sparkle.

Improve your profitability by assigning workers their own telephone code for calls that can't be charged to a client. At the end of each month, deduct the cost of personal calls from their salary.

Allow your children to approach workers directly for causes they're involved with. Point out to your employees how bad your children will feel if they don't win the prize for raising the most money, selling the most cookies or getting a huge number of sponsors for their event.

Help yourself to any of the food in the company refrigerator. If your workers complain, remind them that the only reason the organization has this appliance is due to your generosity as a Human Resource Manager.

Stop your workers from going into debt when they travel by getting them to charge all of their business expenses to their personal credit card. After they receive the bill, have them to submit it, along with their original receipts, to your accounts payable department.

Ask your workers to run a few errands and pick you up something—anything—for your lunch. Complain loudly about whatever items they bring back and state that as a Human Resource Manager you couldn't possibly eat that crap. Then, refuse to pay for the item.

At meetings, get everybody to wear a name tag with their name and personal information on it. This makes it very easy for you to see who is of use to you as a Human Resource Manager, and who isn't.

Whenever you encounter employees holding a conversation, remind them that all discussions are only to take place in officially sanctioned meetings.

If you have an urgent task, spend a lot of time explaining why it's important to you as a Human Resource Manager, exactly how it should be completed, and why it must be on your desk at 9:00 a.m. tomorrow morning.

Never waste time checking business cards before they're printed. Printers have great spelling abilities and the worker can always pay to have their cards reprinted if they're unhappy with the result.

Even if an employee is working on a task in an area that's outside your area of expertise as a Human Resource Manager, feel free to offer input and encouragement. After all, two heads are always better than one.

Make your carpets last longer by insisting that your workers and customers take off their shoes before entering your premises. As well as reducing your future refurbishment costs, you'll spend less on cleaning.

Listen to all of your workers' phone calls, monitor their emails, check their texts and eavesdrop on their conversations. Not only will this expand your knowledge as a Human Resource Manager about your employees, it will come in useful if you ever have to fire the employee.

Protect your workers from evil by opening all mail and packages—including those marked personal—as they enter your premises. Remind your employees that anything delivered to your address belongs to the company.

While your workers are required to conduct all their personal business after work, you as a Human Resource Manager, may sometimes need to handle your personal matters during company hours. Feel free to cut your toenails, iron your clothes or brush your teeth when issuing instructions to your employees.

Reduce the possibility of mistakes by sitting next to an employee as he or she works and issue instructions as they tackle each task. The worker will appreciate your input, because they know that Human Resource Managers possess special skills.

*Reduce your stress levels by delegating unpleasant tasks such as firing workers to your management trainees. They'll not only get the assertiveness training they need, they'll also see how hard your job is.*

Use desktop publishing to the fullest, and show your workers how flexible the technology is, by continuing to edit documents after they've been laid out and approved by the client.

As a Human Resource Manager, you are entitled to take full credit for everything your employees accomplish. After all, it's your existence that makes their jobs possible.

Prevent office leaks by using phones, texts and email as little as possible. Instead, set up face-to-face meetings to discuss every matter—no matter how trivial it may appear.

Help your workers keep their families together by randomly testing everyone for drugs on a monthly basis. Not only will you stop them overdosing, you'll prevent them from wasting their money on illegal substances.

Stay in touch with changing market conditions by instituting frequent employee reorganizations. As a Human Resource Manager, you know how important to keep in touch with what's happening and prevent your workers from becoming complacent about new trends.

Prevent your workers from getting distracted by instating a clean desk policy. Personal photographs and memorabilia can cloud your employees thinking and prevent them from doing their jobs.

Prevent the competition from infiltrating your offices by requiring all of your workers to carry their official company identification at all times. Do not allow employees to enter the premises without their ID—even if you know them personally.

When an employee loses a loved one, show your human side as a Human Resource Manager by casually mentioning how sorry you are to hear about their loss as you pass them in the hallway. Ask the affected employee how this death will affect his or her work.

Never pay for your employees' phone roaming or texting charges while they're traveling. Just about everything can wait until they return home. And if it can't, it's their responsibility, not yours.

Workers have no idea how hard you work as a Human Resource Manager, or the challenges you face on a daily basis. Let them know how easy your job would be if you had competent employees.

Make sure your workers get the most out of every meeting by asking participants random questions throughout the meeting. Before everybody leaves the room, ask an employee at random to summarize all of the important points.

Even though Human Resource Managers can never be proven wrong, if a worker discovers an error in something that you did, make the change and shrug off the comment. Tell the worker that it's only a very small detail and it doesn't change anything.

Improve your company's profitability by implementing changes that failed at your competition. Point out that you have better management, and as a Human Resource Manager, you're confident that your workers will not make the same mistakes.

Stop workers from stealing your money by requiring receipts for every expense they incur, regardless of how small the amount is. If they claim that the local bus service didn't issue a receipt, allow them to submit a notarized statement to this effect.

If you're holding several functions during the week, keep your costs down by having everything delivered on Monday and storing it until needed. Almost all food lasts longer than the caterer claims.

Make all exit interviews personal. Use this final opportunity to point out all of the departing worker's faults and let him or her know that you've been carrying them for years.

Reduce your healthcare costs by choosing a health plan with a high deductible. You don't want your workers rushing to the doctor every time they have a headache or a slight pain.

When you fire a worker, do it after your other employees have gone home. When they see a new person in the former worker's seat the next day, they'll assume your former worker is on vacation.

Give the bathroom key to a trusted employee and get him or her to store it in a locked cabinet. Have your workers sign for the key whenever they need to use the facilities.

To indoctrinate new workers into your company culture, allocate every new employee a mentor. To prevent them picking up bad habits, make sure the mentor works in a different department.

Encourage your workers to save money by eliminating all travel advances. Paying expenses thirty days after they've submitted an expense report allows your employees to deposit the check into their bank account and watch their savings grow.

Book your workers who are traveling alone into a youth hostel to prevent from feeling lonely or isolated. This not only takes their mind off their loneliness, it also helps them make new, younger friends.

Make sure that your clients receive the best possible service by calling them a couple of minutes after you send an email to ensure that they got it. Ask when you'll get a response.

Prevent your workers worrying about their futures by

*Show your management skills by getting your overseas employees to do everything exactly the same way it's done at the head office—regardless of local conditions, laws or customs.*

refusing to comment on rumors—even if they're false. Your employees are never going to believe anything that a Human Resource Manager tells them.

When your workers are traveling, show how compassionate you are as a Human Resource Manager by eliminating the need for them to get receipts for every bus or train fare. Instead have them purchase an unlimited travel card to get from their hotel room to meetings. Not only will this reduce your travel costs, it will allow your employee to explore the city they're visiting after they've finished work.

As a Human Resource Manager it's important to get your point of view across. Do this by speaking for as long as necessary at every meeting. After you've finished, go around the room and get each worker to explain what you said and what they're required to do.

Insist that your workers get their clients to sign a statement after each meeting showing exactly how long the meeting took, and how long they spent with your worker. Many employees use the time after their client meeting finishes to take care of personal business.

Prevent your workers from spending too long in the bathroom by eliminating all janitorial services. Eventually your staff will get the message and clean the bathrooms themselves or do their business before they come to work or after they go home.

Retail employees often give too much change. Eliminate this by deducting shortages from their salary. Charge an additional administrative fee to cover your costs. Use overages to improve your bottom line.

Offer your employees split shifts whenever possible. Workers love having time off in the middle of the day to run errands and recharge their batteries before returning to work for the evening rush.

Help new workers handle their jobs better and acquire new skills by scheduling "voluntary" training sessions at 6:00 a.m. on Sundays. Let those employees who are unable to attend these sessions know how important each meeting is to their continued employment.

When flying with employees, friends or club members remind them how important Human Resource Managers are by purchasing a first-class seat for yourself.

Workers know how to take advantage of your generosity as Human Resource Manager by inflating expenses such as tips for their meals, cab and hotel bills. Eliminate this scam by insisting that your employees to pay for these optional gratuities themselves.

Reduce the costs of your holiday party by holding it just before a critical deadline. Because many workers will be unable to attend, you'll spend less on food and drink, but still get to look good in the eyes of your employees.

Reduce theft by searching your workers' bags each night before they leave the premises. Confiscate anything that could belong to the company if the worker doesn't have a receipt.

Because the food at your company function will be

unwrapped before the workers arrive, purchase generic snacks, day-old meats and leftovers. Your workers will never know the difference and you'll save a fortune.

Prevent your workers from taking advantage of you as a Human Resource Manager by placing a sign-in/ signout sheet outside the bathroom. By monitoring how long every employee spends in the facilities, you can see instantly which employees are wasting time.

Cut training costs by getting all potential employees to complete a one-week, "training course" before making your final decision on whether to hire them. Charge them a fee for course and the upheaval they cause.

Show ex-employees how much money you have as a Human Resource Manager by suing them if they try to work for a competitor. Remind them that they possess your trade secrets and that the court will always side with you.

Since Human Resource Managers hate controversy, the best way to avoid being rushed into a bad decision is to defer anything that could cause trouble until your next meeting.

# AFTERWORD

I started writing this book while I was working for a mid-sized company that was filled with more unhappy employees than I'd ever met. In fact, every person who worked for this organization talked about quitting on a daily basis. Few did.

I thought the owners of this organization had perfected the art of demotivation. I was wrong. After a few years, I moved to another company, that not only demotivated its employees, it also used the same tactics on their clients and friends. Yes, their friends and clients.

Because many of their clients were friends, they knew they wouldn't take their business elsewhere. So, instead of offering them discounts, they charged their friends more. That's right, they charged them extra. Why? Because they could.

How did they get away with this? They knew that their friends would never question their prices, and if they did, they could always explain away the difference (better materials, more skilled employee, computer error, etc.). And if the friend left, well, they weren't really concerned because: "you can't loose a friend you never had."

How could they expect happy workers, when they had demotivated clients and friends? They didn't. Nobody stayed. Their longest-serving employee had ten years service, their second longest—me—had two years.

ost organizations would be concerned about this, ners swept the problem under the carpet. They at there was no such thing as a talented, happy, (all talented employees are bosses).

than trying to motivate their workers with s, raises and incentives, these innovative thinkers 'ated their workers with platitudes and insults. of dealing with the complaints, they tackled the ues—increasing profits, reducing costs and coming ı new ways to squeeze more out of their employees.

he employees would have liked the owners to se with them, it wasn't expected. The owners used their advantage by getting nastier and meaner at pportunity, hoping that their fat, lazy employees walk out the door, so they could be replaced with er, harder working models.

sounds bad, ask yourself: are you in business to friends or to make money? If the answer is to make y, keep reading. If it's to make friends, enroll an motivational seminar so your friends, family and yees can take advantage of you, your niceness and company.

***Geoffrey Young***
***'ork, NY.***
***dolyttle.com***

# ACKNOWLEDGEMENTS

*Assign new employees a mentor to make it easier for them to fit into the company. To keep costs down, make sure the mentor is on a business trip during the new worker's first couple of weeks.*

Writing a book is always a team effort due of the large number of things that need to be done. Until I started this project I had no idea how many people were willing to help me out for free—including those who had absolutely no idea who I was (a very, very big thank you to Dick DeBartolo for writing the foreword).

While I promised to thank everybody, there's no way to avoid missing somebody. So, if you made a contribution to this book, let me know how demotivated you are and I'll include you in the next version.

Because many of the people who helped me out work for organizations that would scream if they knew that their corporate secrets were out in the world, I'm not going to say what anybody actually did, needless to say some people gave me tips, others provided insight and inspiration, while others fed me when I was hungry.

Here's the list (in alphabetical order): Zach Auslander, Dennis Badlyans, Sharon Behnke, Carole Bleicher, Helen Boltson, Hazel Bradley, Zippy Collins, Ben Curry, Andy Clarke, Stephen Colbert, Mark Day, Dick DeBartolo, Nick Denton, Fred Dieckamp, Darlene Durran, William Hammond, Tracee Hines, Ralph Gammon, Ellen Greenberg, Ruth Mostern, John Oakley, Randy Patrick, Shirley Pon, Greg Rapport, Barbara Schancupp, Marvin Schancupp, Pam Schancupp, Carl Schell, David Seto, Jules Smirke, Harvey Spencer, Leslie Spencer, Jon Stewart, Susan Weintraub, Elaine Weiss, Laura Wenzell, Diane Young, Jackson Young, Kristen Young, Mike Young, Robert Young and everybody else who has ever demotivated me.

# The Personalized Edition

If you'd like to make this book your own, why not order a personalized copy for yourself or a friend. Simply go to www.dolyttle.com and order a copy of either The Best Ever Book of YOUR NAME Jokes or The Best Ever Guide to Demotivation for YOUR NAME.

We'll we put your name and picture on the cover and throughout the book. Or, if you'd rather, simply order one of the many titles available

At $19.95 per copy it's a great deal. Simply go to www.dolyttle.com.

# *ORDER! FORM*

Dolyttle & Seamore
198 Garth Road Suite 2D
Scarsdale, NY 10583
212-496-8771 • info@dolyttle.com
(For faster service go to www.dolyttle.com)

Name

Address Apt.

City State ZIP

Country

Email

Phone

**Title:**
The Best Ever Book of ______________________________ Jokes
The Best Ever Guide to Demotivation for ______________________________

If you don't have a friend, don't worry about it. We'll nominate somebody be your friend, at absolutely no additional cost. Each book is $19.95 plus $3.99 shipping for the first book and $2.00 for each additional copy. Call for pricing for large orders and corporate prices.

WWW.DOLYTTLE.COM

On the next couple of pages, you'll see a selection of our current titles. Order either the demotivation book, the joke book or both.

**OCCUPATIONS**

Account Executive, Acccountant, Actor, Acupuncturist, Administrative Assistant, Administrator, Aide, Air Force, Air Traffic Controller, Ambulance Officer, Analyst, Anesthesiologist, Announcer, Antique Dealer, Architect, Army, Assistant, Astronomer, Athlete, Audiologist, Auditor, Author, Baker, Balloon Artist, Banker, Barber, Barista, Bartender, Beautician, Beekeeper, Benefit Manager, Bill Collector, Biologist, Bodybuilder, Book Seller, Bookkeeper, Bricklayer, Builder, Building Manager, Bus Driver, Business Owner, Butcher, Camera Operator, Camp Counselor, Camp Director, Candy Store Owner, Car Salesman, Caregiver, Carpenter, Carpet Layer, Carpet Salesperson, Cartographer, Chauffeur, Chef, Chemical Engineer, Chemist, Chiropractor, Cinematographer, Civil Engineer, Civil Servant, Claims Adjuster, Clerk, Clown, Coach, Coast Guard, Company Director, Compliance Officer, Computer Engineer, Computer Operator, Computer, Programmer, Conductor, Conference Producer, Congressman, Conservationist, Cook, Copy Editor Corrections Officer, Counselor, Courier Criminal, Cyclist, Dancer Data Entry Operator, Debt Collector, Deli Owner, Delivery Person, Dental Assistant, Dental Hygienist, Dental Technician, Dentist, Dermatologist, Designer, Detailer, Detective, Dispatcher, Doctor, Dog Walker, Doorman, Dressmaker, Driver, Drug Dealer, Dry Cleaner, Electrician, Engineer, Engraver, Entertainer, Entrepreneur, Environmental Engineer, Epidemiologist, Episcopalian, Executive, Exporter, Falcons' Fan, Farmer, Fire Fighter, Fireman, Fisherman, Fitness Instructor, Flight Attendant, Flight Engineer, Florist, Flower Seller, Food Technologist, Funeral Director, Furniture Maker, Furniture Salesperson, Garbage Collector, Gardener, Geologist, Golfer, Graphic Designer, Grave Digger, Grocer, Guard, Hairdresser, Handyman, Hardware Store, Owner, Historian, Horticulturist, Host, Hostess, Human Resource, Consultant, Human Resource, Manager, Importer, Industrial Engineer, Information Systems, Manager, Information Technology, Manager, Inspector, Instructor, Intelligence Officer, Interpreter, Janitor, Jeweler, Journalist, Judge, Laborer, Labourer, Landscaper, Law Clerk, Lawyer, Life Guard, Locksmith, Machinist, Magician, Mail Carrier, Mail Sorter, Mailman, Makeup Artist, Manager, Managing Director, Manicurist, Marines, Marriage Counselor, Mathematician, Mechanic, Medical Assistant, Medical Technician, Messenger, Meteorologist, Meter Reader, Midwife, Miner, Minister, Model, Musician, National Guard, Naturalist, Naturopath, Navy, Notary Public, Nuclear Engineer, Nuclear Physicist, Nurse, Nursing Aide, Obstetrician, Occupational Therapist, Optician, Orthodontist, Paralegal, Parking Inspector, Parole Officer, Party Planner, Payroll Clerk, Pediatric Oncologist, Pediatrician, Pharmacist, Pharmacy, Technician, Philosopher, Physical Therapist, Physician, Physician's Assistant, Physician's Assistant, Physicist, Physiotherapist, Pilot, Plumber, Podiatrist, Police, Political Scientist, Postal Carrier, Postal Worker, Postman, Postmaster, Potter, PR Executive, President, Priest, Printer, Prison Guard, Prison Officer, Probation Officer, Producer, Professor, Programmer, Projectionist, Proofreader, Prostitute, Psychiatric Nurse, Psychiatrist, Psychic, Psychologist, Public Servant, Purchasing Manager, Rabbi, Radiographer, Radiologist, Real Estate, Refrigeration Mechanic, Registrar, Repairman, Reporter, Roofer, Rubbish Collector, Sailor, Sales Manager Joke, Salesman, Salesperson, Scientist, Secretary, Security Guard Joke, Senator, Sheriff, Shoemaker, Shop Assistant, Sign Writer, Singer, Skin Care Specialist, Small Business Owner, Social Worker, Socialist, Sociologist, Sound Technician, Speech Therapist, Spy, Statistician, Student, Subeditor, Superintendent, Surfer, Surgeon, Surveillance Officer, Surveyor, Swimmer, Swimming Instructor, Tailor, Taxi Driver, Teacher, Teaching Assistant, Technician, Technologist, Technology Writer, Telemarketer, Therapist, Ticket Collector, Tire Dealer, Tire Technician, Title Examiner, Tour Guide, Trainer, Travel Agent, Truck Driver, Tutor, Tyre Dealer, Tyre Technician, Umpire, Undertaker, Underwriter, Upholsterer, Urban Planner, Urologist, Usher, Veterinarian, Waiter, Waitress, Web Designer, Welder, Window Washer, Zookeeper, Zoologist

**NATIONALITIES**

Afghan, Albanian, Algerian, American, Andorran, Angolan, Anguillan, Antiguan, Argentinean, Armenian, Australian, Austrian, Azerbaijani, Bahamian, Bahraini, Bangladeshi, Barbadian, Batswana, Belarusian, Belgian, Belizean, Beninese, Bermudian, Bhutanese, Bolivian, Bosnian, Brazillian, British, Bruneian, Bulgarian, Burkinabe, Burmese, Burundian, Cambodian, Cameroonian, Canadian, Cape Verdian, Caymanian, Central African, Chadian, Chilean, Chinese, Christmas Islander, Cocos Islander, Colombian, Comoran, Congolese, Costa Rican, Croat, Cuban, Cypriot, Czech, Danish, Djibouti, Dominica, Dutch, East Timorese, Ecuadorean, Egyptian, Emirati, English, Equatoguinean, Eritrean, Estonian, Ethiopian, Falkland Islander, Fijian, Filipino, Finnish, French, Gabonese, Gambian, Georgian, German, Ghanaian, Gibraltarian, Greek, Greenlander, Grenadian, Guadeloupian, Guatemalan, Guianese, Guinea-Bissauan, Guinean, Guyanese, Haitian, Herzegovinian, Honduran, Hungarian, Icelandic, Indian, Indonesian, Iraqi, Irish, Israeli, Italian, Jamaican, Japanese, Jordanian, Kazakhstani, Kenyan, Kiribati, Kittian, Korean, Kuwaiti, Kyrgyzstani, Laotian, Latvian, Lebanese, Liberian, Libyan, Liechtensteiner, Lithuanian, Luxembourger, Macedonian, Madagascan, Mahorais, Malagasy, Malawian, Malaysian, Maldivian, Malian, Maltese, Marshallese, Martinican, Mauritanian, Mauritian, Mexican, Micronesian, Moldovan, Monacan, Mongolian, Montenegrin, Montserratian, Moroccan, Mozambican, Myanmarese, Namibian, Nauruan, Nepalese, Netherlander, Nevisian, New Zealand, New Zealander, Nicaraguan, Niger, Nigerian, Nigerien, Norwegian, Omani, Pakistani, Palauan, Palestinian, Panamanian, Papua, New Guinean, Paraguayan, Peruvian, Polish, Portuguese, Puerto Rican, Qatari, Reunionese, Romanian, Russian, Rwandan, Saint Helenian, Saint Lucian, Saint Vincentian, Salvadoran, Sammarinese, Sao Tomean, Saudi Arabian, Scottish, Senegalese, Serbian, Seychellois, Sierra Leonean, Singaporean, Slovakian, Slovene, Solomon Islander, Somali, Somalian, South African, Spaniard, Spanish, Sri Lankan, Sudan, Sudanese, Surinamer, Swazi, Swedish, Swiss, Syrian, Taiwanese, Tajik, Tanzanian, Thai, Tobagonian, Togolese, Tongan, Trinidadian, Tunisian, Turkish, Turkmen, Tuvaluan, Ugandan, Ukrainian, Uruguayan, Uzbekistani, Vanuatu, Venezuelan, Vietnamese, Virgin Islander, Welsh, Yemeni, Zambian, Zimbabwean and others

**SPORTS**

Adventure, Archery, Badminton, Athlete, Baseball, Basketball, Bodybuilder, Bowling, Boxing, Canoeist, Coach, Cricket, Cyclist, Dancer, Diving, Fencing, Fisherman, Fitness Instructor Football, Golfer, Gymnast, Handball, Hiking, Hockey, Horse Riding, Hunting, Jockey, Kayaker, Mountaineer, Orienteering, Pilot, Ping Pong, Polo, Racing, Racquetball, Referee, Rower, Rugby, Runner, Sailor, Skier, Shooter, Soccer Softball, Squash, Surfer, Swimmer, Swimming Instructor, Table Tennis, Trainer, Tramping, Umpire, Volleyball, Weightlifter, Wrestling

**Baseball**

Angels, Astros, Athletics, Blue Jays, Braves, Brewers, Cardinals, Cubs, Diamondbacks, Dodgers, Giants, Indians, Mariners, Marlins, Mets, Nationals, Orioles, Padres, Phillies, Pirates, Rangers, Rays, Red Sox, Reds, Rockies, Royals, Tigers, Twins, White Sox, Yankees

**Baseball**

76ers, Blazers, Bobcats, Bucks, Bulls, Cavaliers, Celtics, Clippers, Grizzlies, Hawks, Heat, Hornets, Jazz, Kings, Knicks, Lakers, Magic, Mavericks, Nets, Nuggets, Pacers, Pistons, Raptors, Rockets, Spurs, Suns, Thunder, Timberwolves, Warriors, Wizards

**American Football**
Football, Soccer, 49ers, Bears, Bengals, Bills, Broncos, Browns, Buccaneers, Cardinals, Chargers, Chiefs, Colts, Cowboys, Dolphins, Eagles, Falcons, Giants, Jaguars, Jets, Lions, Packers, Panthers, Patriots, Raiders, Rams, Ravens, Redskins, Saints, Seahawks, Steelers, Texans, Titans, Vikings

**English Football / English Soccer**
Football, Soccer, Arsenal, Aston Villa, Chelsea, Everton, Fulham, Liverpool, Manchester City, Manchester United, Newcastle United, Norwich City, Queens Park, Rangers, Reading, Southampton, Stoke City, Sunderland, Swansea City, Tottenham Hotspur, West Bromwich, Albion, West Ham United, Wigan Athletic

**SEXUAL**
Gay, Homosexual, Lesbian, Masturbator, Nudist, Pervert, Prostitute, Transsexual, Wanker

**MEDICAL**
Acupuncturist, Ambulance Officer, Anesthesiologist Biologist, Chemist, Chiropractor, Counselor, Dental Assistant, Dental Hygienist, Dental Technician, Dermatologist, Doctor, Naturopath, Nurse, Nursing Aide, Obstetrician, Occupational Therapist, Optician, Orthodontist, Pediatric Oncologist, Pediatrician, Pharmacist, Pharmacy, Technician, Physician, Physician's Assistant Joke, Physical Therapist, Podiatrist, Physiotherapist, Psychiatric Nurse, Psychologist, Psychiatrist, Radiologist, Radiographer, Surgeon, Therapist, Undertaker, Urologist, Veterinarian

**GENERAL**
Blind, Blond, Boy Scout, Brunette, Cat Lover, Conservationist, Criminal, Dog Lover, Drug Dealer, Essex Girl, Girl Scout, Pilot, Redhead, Redneck, Vegan, Vegetarian

**CREATIVE**
Actor, Artist, Author, Balloon Artist, Cinematographer, Clown, Conductor, Dancer, Designer, Dressmaker, Entertainer, Graphic Designer, Hat Maker, Pilot, Singer, Woodworker, Writer

**RELIGION**
Atheist, Baptist, Born Again, Buddhist, Catholic, Christian, Episcopalian, Jehovah's Witness, Jewish, Mormon, Muslim, Pagan, Protestant, Scientologist, Witch, Unitarian

**POLITICAL**
Barack Obama, Christian Democrat, Communist, Congressman, Conservative, Criminal, Democrat, Glenn Beck, Independent, Labour, Liberal, Libertarian, Michael Bloomberg, Michele Bachmann, Mitt Romney, Newt Gingrich, Non-Voter, Republican, Senator, Social Democrat, Socialist, Tea Party

6612101R00060

Printed in Great Britain
by Amazon.co.uk, Ltd.,
Marston Gate.